WONDERS
OF THE **WORLD**

The Easter
Island Statues

Other books in the Wonders of the World series include:

The Easter Island Statues

Deborah Underwood

KIDHAVEN PRESS

An imprint of Thomson Gale, a part of The Thomson Corporation

Detroit • New York • San Francisco • San Diego • New Haven, Conn.
Waterville, Maine • London • Munich

THOMSON

★ ™

GALE

LIBRARY OF CONGRESS CATALOGING-IN-PUBLICATION DATA

Underwood, Deborah.
  The Easter Island statues / by Deborah Underwood.
    p. cm. — (Wonders of the world)
  Includes bibliographical references and index.
  ISBN 0-7377-3065-X (hard cover : alk. paper)
  1. Megalithic monuments—Easter Island—Juvenile literature. 2. Easter Island—History—Juvenile literature. 3. Easter Island—Antiquities—Juvenile literature. I. Title. II. Wonders of the world (KidHaven Press)
  F3169.U63 2004
  996.1'8—dc22   2004012062

Printed in the United States of America

CONTENTS

Land of the Stone Giants

On Easter Day in 1722, Dutch sea captain Jacob Roggeveen and his fleet of three ships came upon a tiny, uncharted island in the Pacific Ocean. Roggeveen named it Paasch Eyland, which means "Easter Island" in Dutch. The enormous statues that dotted the island mystified Roggeveen. The statues, called **moai** by the natives, were so large that they could be seen from his ships.

Today the statues of Easter Island still fill visitors with awe. Hundreds of the human-shaped figures loom over the island's rolling hills. Some stand in solemn rows atop carefully crafted rock platforms. Shifting soil has buried others up to their chins. Still others lie unfinished in a crater of a volcano, as though awaiting the return of the people who began carving them so long ago.

The statues on Easter Island are unique. Although carved stone figures can be found on other Pacific islands, none match the size of the Easter Island statues.

Easter Island's stone statues are the largest carved stone figures on any Pacific island.

Easter Island

ASIA

NORTH AMERICA

Atlantic Ocean

Pacific Ocean

Indian Ocean

AUSTRALIA

Easter Island

SOUTH AMERICA

A row of stone statues, called moai, stands along Easter Island's rocky coastline.

The statues range in size from about 6 feet to more than 30 feet (1.83 meters to 9.14 meters) tall. The largest moai yet discovered was never finished. It would have stood about 70 feet (21.34 meters) tall and weighed more than 150 tons (136 metric tons)!

An Isolated Island

Easter Island is one of the most remote inhabited islands on earth. It is part of the Polynesian Islands, a group found in the Pacific Ocean. Easter Island lies more than 1,100 miles (1,770 kilometers) from its nearest neighbor, Pitcairn Island, and 2,300 miles (3,701 kilometers) from the western coast of South America. Although some still call it Easter Island, those who live there prefer the island's Polynesian name, Rapa Nui.

Rapa Nui was created by the eruptions of three undersea volcanoes. The volcanoes erupted at different times, but the lava from them joined together to form the island. Rapa Nui is shaped like a triangle, with a volcano at each point. However, the volcanoes have not erupted for thousands of years, and freshwater lakes fill some of the volcanic craters and cones.

The island is only about 63 square miles (163 square kilometers)—just a tiny speck in the enormous Pacific Ocean. Four Easter Islands would easily fit inside New York City. The longest side of the island is a mere 13 miles (21 kilometers) long. The landscape is swept by near-constant winds.

The Statues of Rapa Nui

The massive stone statues that populate Rapa Nui have intrigued visitors for hundreds of years. Nearly nine hundred moai have been found on the island. Others may still be buried in the earth.

Although the statues are alike in appearance, no two are exactly the same. The moai are upright, humanlike figures with large heads and bodies that end at the hips. The statues have prominent noses and lips. Each figure holds its arms at its sides, but its long, narrow fingers wrap around to meet in front of its abdomen.

How Big Is a Moai?

Height in feet

20

15

10

5

0

A small moai	Girl	A large moai
6 feet	5 feet 4 inches	20 feet

Archaeologists replace the coral and stone eyes that long ago fell from the eye sockets of these moai.

The moai were carved from a type of volcanic rock called **tuff**. Tuff is formed when volcanic ash hardens and compresses. Tuff is a fairly soft stone, but as it is exposed to weather, it becomes very hard.

Hollow sockets mark the places where the statues' eyes would be. It was once thought that the eye sockets of the statues were meant to be empty. However, in 1978 archaeologist Sonia Haoa found pieces of white coral and a red stone beneath a fallen statue. The coral and stone fit together perfectly to form an eye. Experts now think all the moai that stood on the ceremonial platforms once had eyes. They believe that eyes were inserted into the carved eye sockets during special ceremonies. Putting in the eyes may have been a way of awakening the statues and activating their **mana**, or spiritual powers.

A moai head lies on a grassy slope near the Rano Raraku quarry. Many unfinished moai rest along the quarry's slopes.

Between sixty and one hundred of the moai were topped with red cylinders of carved stone. These headpieces were mentioned in the records kept by Jacob Roggeveen and other early visitors to the island. They are known as topknots, or **pukao**. Some believe the pukao represent a particular hairstyle worn by the people of Rapa Nui. Others think they are meant to represent feather headdresses worn by the island's warriors.

The Moai Factory

On the eastern part of Rapa Nui sits a large volcanic cone called Rano Raraku. Rano Raraku was formed by the eruption of Maunga Terevaka, the island's largest volcano. The inside of the crater slopes gently down to a reedy lake at the bottom. Plants and grasses cover patches of ground both inside and outside the crater.

Nearly all of the island's moai were carved in Rano Raraku. It was chosen as the main quarry because the volcanic rock there was suitable for statue carving. Statues were carved from the rock both inside and outside the crater walls.

Today about four hundred statues can still be found inside the crater and resting on the grassy slopes outside. Some of the statues are only half-visible. Over time they have been buried by dirt washing down the mountain. Some of the moai in Rano Raraku are finished. Others are only partly carved.

Mysteries of the Moai

From the time that outsiders first arrived on Rapa Nui, the island's statues have puzzled visitors to the island.

Over the years numerous researchers have come to the island to try to answer questions about the moai and the people who created them.

Some scientists have focused on the moai themselves. Every moai on the island has been carefully measured and entered into a database. Researchers have mapped the locations of all the statues on the island. They have performed many experiments to try to learn how the statues were carved and transported.

Others have tried to understand the society that created the statues. The people of Rapa Nui had no written language during the time the moai were carved. Historians have had to rely on information from interviews with the islanders themselves. Some of the stories islanders told are mentioned in the logs of ships that visited the island in the eighteenth and nineteenth centuries. In the last hundred years researchers traveled to Rapa Nui specifically to collect the stories passed down by its people.

The statue carving on Rapa Nui ended hundreds of years ago. However, by studying the moai, the other structures on the island, and the islanders' stories, scholars have pieced together a picture of the island's ancient culture.

CHAPTER TWO

Who Made the Statues?

The first settlers arrived on Rapa Nui more than a thousand years ago. For many years scholars disagreed about whether these settlers sailed east from another Polynesian island or west from South America. Experts have now determined that the settlers traveled from Polynesia.

No one knows for sure why the original settlers left their homeland or how they found Rapa Nui. However stories passed down through generations of people on Rapa Nui give some clues about the island's first people.

The Arrival of Hotu Matu'a

Legends tell that the first settler of Rapa Nui was a powerful chief named Hotu Matu'a, which means "great parent." In some versions of the story, he left his old home after losing a battle. In others, he was forced to

This Rapa Nui man and young boy are modern-day descendants of the natives who carved the giant moai.

leave after his island sank into the sea. A member of his tribe dreamed of a beautiful land where the chief could make his home, and Hotu Matu'a and his extended family set off to find it. Their settlement party may have included dozens of people or perhaps more than one hundred. Like other Polynesian seafarers, they traveled in large double canoes.

Since the settlers did not know what they would find when they got to their new home, they carried everything they would need to begin their new lives. They packed food and water for the journey. They also brought plants, animals, and tools. Live chickens made the trip with them, as did another popular source of food, Polynesian rats. They may have brought pigs and dogs, too. But if so, those animals did not survive long on the island.

Skilled Navigators

Researchers do not know whether the first settlers found Rapa Nui by chance or whether they knew it existed and traveled to it on purpose. It is certain that Polynesians were very skilled sea navigators. They paid careful attention to the natural world around them. They used the stars to guide their canoes at night. During the day they watched the sea and the clouds. They knew that ocean waves change their patterns when an island is nearby. Certain cloud patterns also told them when land was near, even if the land itself was too far away to see. Seabirds often head for land as the sun sets, so perhaps a flock of birds led the settlers to their new home.

Island Life

After the settlers arrived on Rapa Nui, they planted sweet potatoes, taros, bananas, yams, and sugarcane. When they arrived the island was covered with a seemingly endless supply of palm trees. They cut and burned away the trees and the island's other native plants to make more room for their food crops. The people built garden enclosures near their homes. Sometimes walls were built around the gardens, and sometimes the gardens were sunk into the earth. This helped protect the plants from the island's strong winds.

The people also ate chicken and fish. The remains of more than a thousand stone chicken houses have been

The Polynesians who settled Rapa Nui used wooden canoes similar to this one to fish the island's waters.

found on the island, so it appears that chickens were an important source of food for the people of Rapa Nui. By looking at the bones in centuries-old garbage piles, scientists discovered that the people of Rapa Nui also ate porpoises.

Their reliable sources of food allowed the people of Rapa Nui to prosper for nearly a thousand years. Their society was organized into **clans**, or family groups. This social system was typical on Polynesian islands. Islanders told archaeologist Katherine Routledge, who studied Rapa Nui in 1914 and 1915, that there had been ten different clans on the island. Each clan was linked to a certain area. However, the divisions between clans were not strict. The clans traded with each other, and people often married outside their clan.

According to legend the clans began when Hotu Matu'a divided up the island. He had six sons and gave each a part of the island to rule. Over time land divisions were changed and more clans were formed. The ruler of the highest-ranking clan was considered to be the island's spiritual leader. The people believed he was a direct descendant of the gods.

Ceremonial Platforms

Between A.D. 1000 and A.D. 1100 the people of Rapa Nui began to build stone platforms called **ahu**. Ahu are similar to outdoor platforms on other Polynesian islands. There are more than three hundred ahu on Rapa Nui. The platforms are rectangular in shape, and vary greatly in size. Some are quite small, and some are more than 300 feet (91.44 meters) long—longer than three basketball courts placed end to end.

An ahu holds moai of different sizes. In front of the
ahu is a stone plaza where people participated in
ceremonies.

The platforms were made by piling up rubble, and
then building stone walls around the pile and adding a
stone top. Some of the walls were made from uncut stones,
but some were very carefully crafted. The sea-facing wall
of an ahu is usually very steep and straight. On the side
of the ahu facing inland, a stone ramp leads up to the top
of the platform. In front of many ahu is a plaza or gath-
ering place. People gathered at the platforms and the areas near them to take part in ceremonies.

Many ahus were built near the ocean. There are large
platforms about every half mile (0.8 kilometers) around

the coast of Rapa Nui. Most of the ahu are parallel to the coastline. Some marked the dividing lines between clan territories. The island's most impressive platforms are called *image ahu*. These platforms were built to hold the very large moai.

Living Faces

For at least five hundred years the people of Rapa Nui spent much time and energy carving the enormous moai. The statues represented honored ancestors who had died. Another name for the moai is *aringa ora*, which means "living faces." The islanders believed that the ancestors possessed a kind of spiritual power called

The islanders carved moai to represent respected ancestors and as a way to channel their spiritual power.

mana. They hoped that if they carved a statue to represent a respected ancestor, the ancestor's mana would enter the statue.

All the statues on the image ahu faced in toward settlements. This way the powerful ancestors could keep watch over the people and their land. The statues were placed on the platforms because the moai bridged the gap between earth and heaven and between the living and the dead.

Researchers may never completely understand the role of the statues in Rapa Nui society. However, the great number of moai proves that the statues were very important to the islanders. The statues appear to have been memorials to great leaders as well as a way to bring the powers of gods and dead ancestors down to earth.

CHAPTER THREE

Carving and Moving the Moai

Carving and moving the moai was a tremendous accomplishment for the Rapa Nui people. Even with modern equipment, moving tons of stone can be a tricky and dangerous business. Yet the islanders managed to move statues all over the island using only wood, rope, and stones.

The moai quarry at Rano Raraku contains hundreds of statues. Some of these moai are finished, but work on others had just started before the carving was halted. Because they can study statues in various stages of the carving process, researchers have a very good idea about how the people of Rapa Nui carved the moai. However, many questions remain about how the finished statues were moved into their places on ahu around the island.

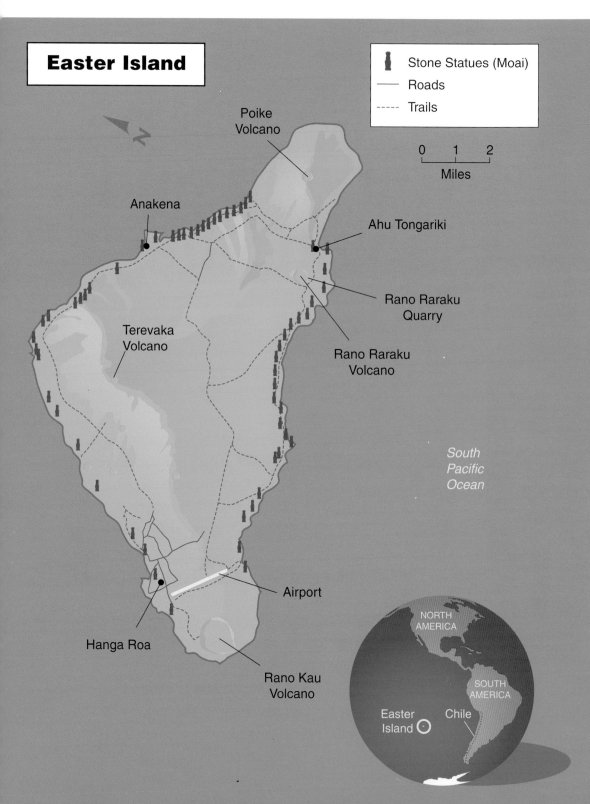

Easter Island

Stone Statues (Moai)
Roads
Trails

0 1 2
Miles

N

Poike
Volcano

Anakena

Ahu Tongariki

Rano Raraku
Quarry

Terevaka
Volcano

Rano Raraku
Volcano

South
Pacific
Ocean

Airport

Hanga Roa

Rano Kau
Volcano

NORTH
AMERICA

SOUTH
AMERICA

Easter
Island

Chile

Honored Stonecutters

From interviews with islanders during the last two hundred years, experts know that carving the moai was sacred and important work. It is likely that ceremonies took place many times during the carving of each statue to bless the work and those who performed it.

The master stonecutters who carved the moai were honored members of society. Alfred Métraux, a scholar from Switzerland, visited Rapa Nui in 1934 to study its ancient culture. People living on the island then told him that the statue carvers had been a privileged class. Even earlier, in the late 1800s, records show that the descendants of the statue carvers referred to their ancestors with as much pride as if they had been royalty.

The stonecutters probably had no responsibilities other than carving the statues. Other people on the island caught fish and grew food to feed them. The remains of many houses have been found in and around Rano Raraku. It is likely that the people who carved the statues lived in these houses.

Carving the Statues

The people of Rapa Nui had no metal tools. However, Rano Raraku's volcanic tuff is soft enough that workers could use sharpened stone picks to carve it. These picks are called **toki**. Toki are made of basalt, which is a dark, hard volcanic rock. Hundreds of toki still can be found scattered throughout the quarry at Rano Raraku.

The moai were carved right into the walls of the quarry at Rano Raraku. They were only removed after most of the carving was completed.

The moai were carved lying on their backs. Workers first used toki to chip away an outline of the statue. Then

One of the many half-buried heads near Rano Raraku crater. Only completed moai were transported from the quarry.

This smoothly shaped rock in the quarry wall is actually a moai abandoned during the first stages of carving.

they continued to shape the statue. They left a long, narrow strip of rock running along the back of the moai, from its head to its foot. Most of the moai were carved while they were still attached to the ground by this strip of stone.

When the statue was nearly finished, the carvers propped up the moai with rocks so that it would not fall over. Then they slowly chipped away its stone strip.

Once the moai was separated from the ground, the workers slid it down the outer slope of Rano Raraku. At the bottom the statue was placed upright in a hole in the ground so its back could be carved. When carving was finished the workers polished the moai with coral to make its surface smooth. Sometimes they carved tattoo-like designs on the finished statues.

The steep slope of Rano Raraku shows how difficult it must have been to move the moai from the quarry.

Moving the Moai

The moai were carved to stand on the ahu that circled the island. This means that the people of Rapa Nui needed to move each statue from the quarry to its platform. Sometimes this involved moving a statue more than 6 miles (9.66 kilometers). An average moai weighs 10 tons (9 metric tons)—about the weight of seven cars. The difficulties involved in moving anything that heavy are considerable. Not only did the islanders need to move the statues, but they needed to move them without harming them. Tuff is fragile, and too many bumps or jolts would have damaged the moai.

Many Theories

Researchers have many theories about how the islanders moved the statues. Island legends say that the statues were so full of mana that they walked into place by themselves. Because of these stories some scientists believe the moai were moved while in an upright position. Others think the statues were placed on their backs or fronts and tied to wooden sleds. These sleds were pulled over rollers or wooden tracks on the ground. The moai may have been loaded onto rafts and floated around the island to their final destinations, but most experts think this is unlikely.

Roads still lead from Rano Raraku to areas on the island where people lived, and the moai were probably transported on these roads. Nearly one hundred fallen statues can be found along the island's roads, so some moai never reached their destinations. Some were broken in transit, so it is clear that no method of moving the statues worked perfectly.

Modern Experiments

During the past fifty years, researchers have tried various ways of moving the heavy stone figures in hopes of learning more about how the moai were moved. In the 1950s Norwegian explorer Thor Heyerdahl supervised a moai-moving test on Rapa Nui. An actual moai was tied to a forked tree branch. One hundred and eighty islanders pulled on ropes to drag it over the ground. They were able to move it a short distance. However, dragging a fragile statue over miles of uneven ground would almost certainly ruin it.

Geologist Charles Love supervised a test to move an upright concrete figure in 1987. He attached two wooden logs to the statue's base, like skis. The figure was then pulled over a series of logs that acted as rollers. A group of twenty-five men easily pulled the 10-ton (9 metric tons) statue 142 feet (43.28 meters). One advantage of moving a statue upright is that its position does not need to be changed once it arrives at its destination. From a distance a statue moved in this way does appear to be walking, just as the legends report.

A Recent Effort

In 1998 archaeologist Jo Anne Van Tilburg and a team of other scientists conducted an experiment on Rapa Nui. They used a 13-foot-tall (3.96 meters) concrete moai that weighed 10 tons (9 metric tons). This statue was designed to be an accurate moai copy.

Researchers take measurements of a moai to feed into a computer model. The model will help them understand how the statues may have been moved.

The researchers not only tried to move the moai over level ground, but they also tried to get it up onto a platform. Dozens of native people were recruited to help. They first tried pulling the statue, lying flat, on a sled over log rollers. However, the rollers did not roll smoothly. So the team attached four rollers to the sled and successfully pulled that over a wooden track of more logs. The advantage of this method is that a statue lying down is more stable than an upright one.

Moving the Moai

Here are three theories about how the moai may have been moved.

1. Moving Moai from Quarry

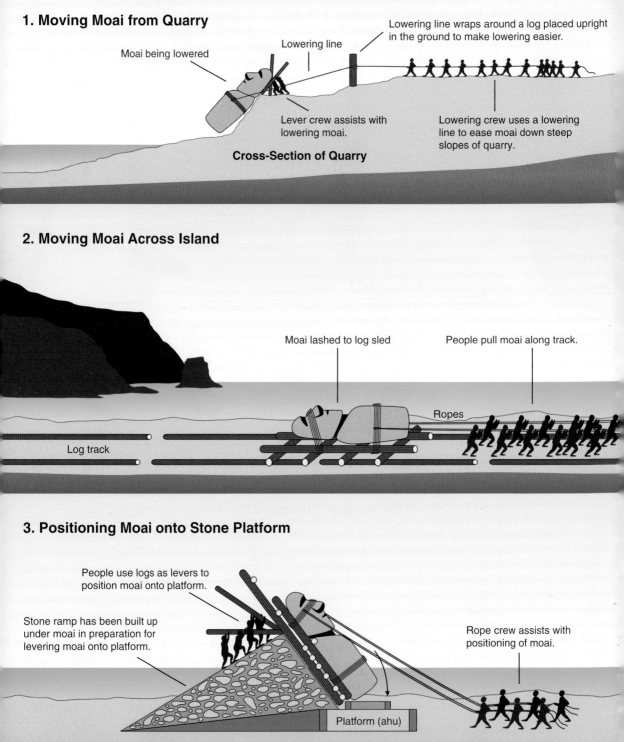

Moai being lowered

Lowering line

Lowering line wraps around a log placed upright in the ground to make lowering easier.

Lever crew assists with lowering moai.

Lowering crew uses a lowering line to ease moai down steep slopes of quarry.

Cross-Section of Quarry

2. Moving Moai Across Island

Moai lashed to log sled

People pull moai along track.

Ropes

Log track

3. Positioning Moai onto Stone Platform

People use logs as levers to position moai onto platform.

Stone ramp has been built up under moai in preparation for levering moai onto platform.

Rope crew assists with positioning of moai.

Platform (ahu)

Source: NOVA Online Web site, *Secrets of Easter Island*.

The experimenters then raised the statue onto a platform. A stone ramp was built leading up to the top of the platform. Using ropes and levers, the team pulled the statue up to the platform. Then the moai had to be raised from a horizontal position to a vertical one. The team used long, wooden poles as levers beneath the statue. Rocks were placed under the statue to prop it up as it was raised. The work was slow and dangerous. As the number of rocks under the statue grew, the rock pile became less stable. Workers had to stand on this unstable pile in order to keep the poles under the statue. It took three days to raise the statue into a standing position.

Mysteries Remain

Scientists will never know for certain how the statues were moved, but these experiments help them learn how well some methods might have worked. It is likely that different methods were used for different situations. One thing is certain: Moving the statues required wood. Trees were needed to supply the wood for rollers, sleds, levers, and tracks across the island. However, by the time the first Europeans arrived, not a single tall tree could be found anywhere on the island. Researchers think the disappearance of the trees contributed to problems that ultimately brought the statue carving to a halt.

CHAPTER FOUR

The End of Statue Carving

Rapa Nui society thrived for hundreds of years. The population grew from the first small group of settlers to perhaps as many as ten thousand people. As the population increased, so did moai production. Over time the people began to make larger and larger statues. They may have hoped that larger moai would bring them more spiritual power, or they may have simply been trying to outdo neighboring clans.

Both the population growth and the increase in statue carving put a strain on the island's limited resources. A period of drought may have contributed to food shortages. Ironically, as food started to become scarce, the people may have poured even more resources into making statues. They may have hoped bigger moai would convince their ancestors and the gods to help them through this difficult time. Moving larger statues

Several moai line a treeless slope of Rano Raraku. Building so many statues strained the island's limited resources.

A view of Rapa Nui shows its treeless landscape. Once its trees were gone, living on the island became difficult.

may have required even more trees. Soon the people of Rapa Nui were confronted with a huge problem: the loss of the trees that had once blanketed their island.

Vanishing Trees

By the time Jacob Roggeveen arrived on Rapa Nui in 1722, all the island's tall trees were gone. The palms that once covered the island grew scarce and then disappeared completely. The **deforestation**, or loss of trees, on Rapa Nui was ultimately disastrous for the people.

Scientists believe that several factors contributed to the island's deforestation. Humans chopped down the palm trees for many reasons. Logs were needed to move the statues and build canoes. The people burned the wood from the trees as fuel. Trees were also cleared to make room for crops.

Humans may have chopped down the trees, but the rats the settlers brought to the island prevented new trees from growing. Palm trees grow from palm nuts. The type of palm that forested Rapa Nui grows from nuts that can take more than a year to **germinate**, or sprout. This long germination period gave rats plenty of time to find the nuts and gnaw on them. Nearly all of the palm nuts discovered on Rapa Nui have been chewed by rats. They were too badly damaged to sprout and grow.

An archaeologist studies a moai head. Many scientists visit the island to study the moai.

The loss of trees led to food shortages. Without trees to anchor it, the island's rich topsoil washed away into the sea. Growing crops became more difficult. Another food source was lost when the birds that were once plentiful on the island fled, possibly in search of trees in which they could nest.

Even fishing was affected by the deforestation. People did not have the wood to build the large, strong canoes they needed to go fishing far out at sea where the porpoises lived. So yet another source of protein was lost.

Once the island's trees were gone, the people of Rapa Nui may have wanted to leave the island in search of a more inviting home. However a long ocean voyage would have required big canoes. Rapa Nui's people were stranded on the island.

Island at War

The people of Rapa Nui appear to have lived in peace for a thousand years. But as food became scarce, clans began to fight with one another. Archaeologists have determined that very few weapons existed on the island until the eighteenth century. Then weapons made of volcanic rock became abundant.

Threats to the Social Structure

As fighting became more common, the old social structure crumbled. Traditional clan leaders were replaced by warlords. These warlords rose to power because of their achievements in battle, not because of who their ancestors were. Experts believe that many people tried to

Most moai were knocked over or destroyed during conflict on the island. The moai shown here have been restored.

A 1960 tidal wave swept away the statues at Ahu Tongariki, but workers returned them to their platforms using cranes.

escape the fighting. They abandoned their homes and sought refuge in the island's numerous caves.

Since the moai were important symbols for the islanders, the statues were natural targets for violence. Warring clans pulled over each other's moai, one by one. Sometimes a sharp rock was placed on the ground near the moai, so that as the statue fell, its neck would break and its head would fall off. By the 1860s not a single moai was left standing on the island.

When outsiders discovered the island, they brought another set of problems. Passing ships infected islanders with diseases such as smallpox and tuberculosis. Slave traders kidnapped Rapa Nui's people and took them to work in South America. By the end of the nineteenth century only about a hundred people survived on the island. The sharp decline in population meant the answers to many questions about the island and its culture were lost.

Restoring the Statues

Today Rapa Nui is part of Chile. Despite its isolation, Rapa Nui is a popular spot for tourists. Thousands of people travel there each year to see its famous statues. The United Nations declared Rapa Nui a World Heritage List site in 1995.

About fifty of the Rapa Nui moai have been restored and returned to their platforms. Universities, the governments of Chile and Japan, and private groups have helped pay for these restorations. Even using modern equipment such as cranes, moving the moai is difficult and time-consuming.

Nature's Toll

The platform called Ahu Tongariki holds the largest group of restored statues. A powerful tidal wave in 1960 swept this ahu's fifteen fallen moai several hundred feet inland. In the early 1990s archaeologist Claudio Cristino supervised the project to restore them. The heads of the moai were reattached with cement, and the statues were placed back on their ahu by workers using giant cranes. Tongariki's impressive, long row of moai makes it a favorite tourist spot.

Because they have been exposed to wind and rain for so long, the moai are crumbling and cracking. Scientists in Germany are developing a chemical treatment to help preserve the stones and prevent further damage. If these treatments are successful, Rapa Nui's magnificent moai may continue to fill visitors with wonder for the next thousand years.

Glossary

ahu (AH-hoo): A stone platform or altar.

clans: Family groups.

deforestation: The cutting down of trees.

germinate: To sprout, like a seed.

mana (MAH-nah): Spiritual power that supposedly filled the moai.

moai (MOE-eye): Rapa Nui's stone statues.

pukao (poo-KOW): The red rock headpieces that some of the statues wore.

toki: Stone picks made of basalt that were used to carve the moai.

tuff: A type of rock made from compressed volcanic ash.

For Further Exploration

Books

Caroline Arnold, *Easter Island: Giant Stone Statues Tell of a Rich and Tragic Past*. New York: Clarion, 2000. Introduction to Easter Island history and culture, with many photographs of the statues and other artifacts.

Kathy Pelta, *Rediscovering Easter Island: How History Is Invented*. Minneapolis: Lerner, 2001. Detailed account of interactions between Easter Island and the outside world, including various visits made by researchers to study the statues.

Web Sites

Easter Island Foundation (www.islandheritage.org). The Easter Island Foundation promotes research on Easter Island and works to preserve its cultural heritage.

Easter Island Statue Project (www.sscnet.ucla.edu/ioa/eisp/index.htm). This Web site has information about current research on Rapa Nui.

Nova: Secrets of Easter Island (www.pbs.org/wgbh/nova/easter). Nova, a public television show, covered a recent attempt to move a moai onto a platform. This site has lots of information about the move, the moai, and the island itself.

Index

Picture Credits

Cover photo: Paul Kennedy/Lonely Planet Images
© Bob Abraham/CORBIS, 18
© James L. Amos/CORBIS, 12, 31, 37
© Bernard Annebicque/CORBIS SYGMA, 11
© Carlos Barria/Reuters/Landov, 8
Chris Jouan, 8, 10, 24
© Wolfgang Kaehler/CORBIS, 20, 27, 28, 35, 39
Paul Kennedy/Lonely Planet Images, 36
James Lyon/Lonely Planet Images, 7, 26
PhotoDisc, 21
Jan Stromme/Lonely Planet Images, 16, 40
Steve Zmina, 32

About the Author

Deborah Underwood writes nonfiction, fiction, and poetry for children. She grew up in Walla Walla, Washington, and received a bachelor's degree in philosophy from Pomona College in Claremont, California. She now lives in San Francisco. When she is not writing, she enjoys reading and singing in a chamber choir. This is her third book for KidHaven Press.